This book is dedicated to Cathy, who was my inspiration and my life.

W H Booth Jnr

Enjoy the Book
Bill. Booth JNR

The Last of the Vindi Boys

Introduction

This book is based on my and other Vindi Boys' experience of, first, the training ship TS Vindicatrix, and then their own experiences, both at Sharpness and their sea-going life. I will also touch on the illustrious history of TS Vindicatrix – warts and all!

About the Author

I am a Vindi Boy 'til I die. I have, if you like, been there and done that, and survived. God knows why after that food. However, this is my fifth book. I was born of Scotland Road, Great Homer Street in Liverpool 5. One of six children. I joined the Vindi as a fifteen-year-old as a trainee. I then went on to spend six years in the Navy, visiting most of the world. After leaving the Navy I went on to have at least twenty various jobs before joining my wife who set up her own company in 1969.

The business still survives and I hope to continue writing until my sea legs give way.

W H Booth Jnr

Acknowledgements

To the small amount of Vindi Boys who were happy to give me their details and to give me their memories of their days on the Vindi in Sharpness, their first trip nightmares and the thrills of being able to travel the world.

Along with what they went on to do when leaving the Merchant Navy and what they achieved in the one life we are given.

I would also like to thank my mate Frank Leonard for running me around most of the pubs and various venues to promote the book. Cheers.

Another thank you must go to Dougie Mannering who, in all my books published, has been instrumental in supplying most of the photographs while I have been receiving major eye surgery for the last two years, made more difficult due to lockdown, which has made me unable to drive a car for two years.

Thank you all.

Contents

Introduction 2

About the Author 2

Acknowledgements 3

Chapter One – All Before Us 6

Chapter Two – Living the Dream 7

Chapter Three – To Be A Vindi Boy 10

Chapter Four – First Trip to Sea and so on 16

Chapter Five – Vindi Boys Travels 20

Chapter Six – Life Beyond the Gates 29

Chapter Seven – Use It Or Lose It 32

Chapter Eight – Future Recognition 35

Chapter Nine – Vindi Boys Stories Circa 1965-66 36

    Cliffy Woodage 36

    Mick O'Toole, Liverpool, circa 1959 38

    Charlie May, circa 1951-52 41

    Vindi Boy Bill Booth, circa 1965-66 42

Chapter Ten – Vindicatrix, The History 44

Chapter Eleven – The 2021 Vindicatrix Reunion at Sharpness 50

Aerial view of the Vindi, docked at Sharpness and the National Sea Training School Camp above.

Chapter One – All Before Us

My name is Bill Booth and I am a Vindi Boy *forever*. No-one can take that away from me.

As a fifteen-year-old I travelled by train from Liverpool to Sharpness, Gloucester to join the National Sea Training School for eight to ten weeks to do my sea training on a ship moored at Sharpness Docks named the TS Vindicatrix.

From this point on, to me, the ship would forever be called the Vindi and all who sailed in her, to coin a phrase, because she would never leave her berth, were called Vindi Boys. In this book I will give you my experience of being a Vindi Boy along with the small amount of Vindi Boys I could muster.

Chapter Two – Living the Dream

When I left school my dream was to join the Navy, like my dad, Grandad Warburton, and my Uncle Tommy and Uncle Sammy. All of whom were Royal Navy. I hoped to join the Royal Navy but, unfortunately, I was colour blind so my only way to go to sea was by way of the Merchant Navy.

My Grandad John Warburton, who unfortunately I never met because he died so very young at only 38 years old, I say that because his discharge book for a young man which I still have to this day is a virtual time capsule. He was at sea all his life. He only had a short life but what a life. He went to more places in his twenty years at sea than most people today would do on a hundred cruise trips. I was told by my Nan that he was a character. He was fearless. Everyone knew and never crossed John Warby.

I would have loved to have met him but he died before I was born. He was a merchant seaman in his discharge book. All is trips to sea were stamped with a VG, being 'very good'. He sailed on one ship for years.

I am sure it was in my DNA to go to sea and follow him, my dad, Uncle Sammy and Uncle Tommy. After leaving school in 1964 at Roscommon Street School, my first job before I could enrol at the shipping pool at fifteen and seven months was a Venmores Building Contractors at Venmore Street, Anfield. I was there for six to nine months as an apprentice plumber. I loved the job and all the lads. My mate and boss was Billy Walker who was good to me as a young boy. Also Jim Foy and Mr Harris. Too many to mention, a great bunch of lads from there, and I was still only under sixteen.

I was off to Mann Island for last minute instructions, train ticket and paperwork a few days later, nearly sixteen and only five foot odd.

Saying *ta-ra* to Mam and Dad, brothers and sister. My brothers all laughing when I was leaving with my kit bag. I was off.

This challenge at fifteen, a mere child, going on a train for eight weeks so far from home on your own, no mobile phones then, no social media, etc. Just you and now and again you thought *what have I done?* But the way I looked at it, it was an adventure. It was a promise I set myself all those years ago as a young boy on the step in our back yard while chopping wood to sell to survive as a family, that one day I will go to sea and continue the journey that is steeped in my genes. And even if I ever got cold feet, I had to see it through. My parents had sacrificed a lot. They were going to do without any keep money off me for a least three months. Think of that sacrifice to a couple who had six kids with a small wage between them.

I had to complete the course. My dad had just started on the Dock and they had six kids. It was a struggle but I was determined to pass the test and return home a merchant seaman.

My education level was not that of a College Don but what I do have is guts and that never say die attitude. If I put my mind to it I will pass out. I am very driven, have had a strict upbringing by my Mam and Dad, they had morals and gave us what they could afford and it was the best childhood I could have had.

And the schools I went to were very disciplined. If you have discipline in your life you have order, you have loyalty and you have trust. You have all those qualities which in today's world are not always apparent.

Looking out of the train window on my own, heading off to live the dream, not overly intellectual but very streetwise, who had served his apprenticeship in the streets of Liverpool Five, is enough said. And you would have to be good to kid me as a fifteen-year-old.

You can't kid the kid who kidded the kids! It was tattooed into my DNA. I would complete the course and come out the other side. I had to, if only to repay my Mam and Dad's promise to let me go to sea in order for me to live the dream I had nurtured all my life.

Mind you, can you see today's kids doing that? Going to a strange place - without Googling it first – for six to eight weeks? On their own with no mobile phone? I would not see my family for eight weeks. No Skype, I had no mates with me to buzz off.

Five foot odd, a midget really. No stick, no dog, no staff to comfort me. No hundred pound in my pocket to see me through. Maybe I had five bob or so. Could it happen with today's kids? I doubt it. Yet it was all we knew then and technology had not invaded our brains yet and taken over our lives – thank God.

In the distance I can see the railway station. It was early November, late afternoon, when the train pulled into Berkeley Railway Station. It was very quiet but for a few people getting off the train. As I stepped off the train and stood on the station platform, two boys approached me and said in a funny accent *'are you going to the sea training school?'*

I replied, *'you mean the Vindicatrix?'* and they said yes. I had just said the word Vindicatrix for the first time and it would live with me forever.

Just then the bus pulled up and me and these two boys were on our way to a totally new life. Bring it on.

Chapter Three – To Be A Vindi Boy

Once inside the double gate it was a whole new ball game. As we arrived late afternoon we were given some food. Well, let's just imagine it was food. It was vile and took a while to digest. But if I'm honest, it was the last thing on my mind. I was only fifteen and it was a lot to take in. I had been building up to this day for most of my early years and to be honest I was knackered. Even at fifteen the whole day took it out of me. I was right into the billet, head down and gone.

The next day hit me like a ton of bricks. Early call and right out into the bitter cold morning, exercising on the parade ground, doing all kind of strange things with our already tired bodies, which was an experience. Run here, lift this, lift that. Now I am awake!

After exercise, I changed and showered. Well, that's new. What's a shower? Me clean at seven in the morning and then down to breakfast. Up until then I had never had a mate but after walking down to the ship in the dock it was happening quickly.

After a whiff of sea air from the River Severn and the pong from the toilets on the quay, I was ready to join and board the TS Vindicatrix for the first time. Yes, I had arrived. I am now officially a Vindi Boy.

I made my way to the table and went for my breakfast – for what it was – the porridge looked like concrete. The toast was dry and hard and the beans like bullets. The eggs were unreal. Bacon was like a Brillo Pad. The lot was awful. Oh, I forgot, I also got a few cockroaches thrown in with the beans. They must have fell off the deckhead.

I met a Scouser at the table. He was a good way down the table, it must have been at least twenty per table. As the boys were coming and going, I could hear the Scouse accent in the lines of boys waiting to be fed. It was like instant mate. After breakfast we were all told to join our groups.

In my group there were three Scousers. I started talking to John and, you know what, he only comes from my neck of the woods, at the end of Greaty. Right facing the bungalows where my Auntie Lizzie and Auntie Bella live, also my Uncle Jimmy and Timmy. It's looking good now. Bring it on.

After breakfast, if you like, I was starving. We all split up and went to our respective classrooms for catering training and dock training. As I was training one day to become a cook. I, along with my new mate John

McCardle, were in the same group in our section and he was also in the same billet, so happy days.

The training on day one was about settling in, getting to know the layout of the camp and all things Vindicatrix. After the initial shock of breakfast, the lunch was worse. Spuds you could use as weapons, fish cakes with no fish in them, and peas to die for, and last the sweet. Well, I have to say it was my favourite – the Vindi roll.

As a boy my favourite cakes always had raisins, currants, sultanas. All that stuff of Eccles Cakes, Chorley Cakes, etc. My Dad was the same. If my Mam said have one he would have four. Anyway, the Vindi roll was steamed in a rectangular tubular tin and consisted of real soft sponge cake, full of raisins and sultanas. We had it with custard and it was great. But there must have been cockroaches in there disguised as raisins. I do believe they're good for you.

I do believe that every Vindi Boy who ate their meals aboard the Vindi will have consumed thousands of cockroaches over their eight to twelve week stay.

Once all the lessons were over we would embark and all head up on the bank to our billets. I don't recall having to do any more lessons that day.

At that time of year when I was there it was starting to go dark at 4 o'clock. Apart from going down to the main hall for some entertainment I just got on with unpacking and was looking forward to day 2 and some nautical knowledge apparently.

The main hall was a hive of activity most nights. Boxing matches were arranged once the new boys had settled into week one, before the next intake arrived. Some of the games on offer were darts, table tennis, and football was an option. But everyone wanted that so it would have to wait as I was new. Lots of matches were arranged between those outside the camp, etc.

At weekends you could go into Berkeley to the cinema, or you could visit the Flying Angel Seaman's Mission. On Sundays we would go to church which was not everyone's cup of tea, but it was good for the soul. If you were late arriving back at camp you would be under the clock. And if it happened regular you were on your way home.

My mate John McCardle never had the privilege of being sent home. He just done a bunk one night. He just could not hack it. It was a shame really as he was my number one mate. Later I would always bump into him back home, or his brother. But he never got to go away to sea and not only did he leave the camp early, but he also departed this world very young.

We were good mates. He was a real comedian. We had a good few weeks before he went AWOL. Funny all the Scousers on the site stuck together. It was at that time 64-65, either The Beatles or The Stones were up there. But of course, as always it was the Scousers who came out on top. We were a force in those days.

During the days we would do a lot of seamanship tasks, lifeboat drill. We would lower the lifeboats over the side of the ship. It was always a laugh. It was let go after grapes and choks but normally something would happen like the lifeboat would be on its side. We would have billet after billet but generally the days went slow because of the time of year I arrived.

The outdoor sports were not always possible. The cold was not a problem as we thrived on that, especially at six o'clock in the morning in our short shorts and vest. You know you were fit, there was no doubt the food was that bad you probably went home at least a stone lighter. You were fitter because of the fresh air, the exercise and the amount of games you got involved in.

The officers were all different. Some were funny, some very strict, but they all did their jobs. There was no favouritism. Not many ended up at the nurse named Codeine Annie's to get your jabs. We would all get our check-ups and most were fit enough to carry on.

We very rarely seen the Captain and to be his 'tiger' was a cushy job. But we would from time to time do little jobs, like his gardener or some painting and cleaning.

I would always look forward to my Mam's food parcels. I never had many. My parents were not well off.

The days were taken up with learning how to do the jobs you would encounter at sea. You would learn to lay out the table in the correct order from the outside in with your cutlery, also how to serve a passenger, which side of the passenger you had to serve the food, as well as general sailor duties.

You would also have to make sure your dumb waiter is fully equipped. It is in fact your lifeline. It must be fully stocked with all you would require in order to look after the passengers you are likely to have at your tables, somethings for both sittings.

Those boys, like myself, were not only trained in the galley, we were also trained in the saloon. Your cutlery training was normally to do weighing food, grain rice flour, use of various utensils and preparation of various meals. The chefs were very informative, even though some of the ovens, vats, etc were very dated.

The officers, though to us at 15 years old, looked very old. They were probably in their fifties or sixties, which of course, today, is not old. They had all been to sea as serving officers and had no doubt travelled the world and were now passing their skills onto the next generation of merchant seamen.

Some had been on massive ships. When asked, the likes of the Mauretania, Queen Mary, Queen Elizabeth, Rena Del Mar, Queen of Bermuda, Sylvania. Only *chop, chop*, the sun is scorching your eye balls, out, up out your beds now, *chop, chop*. Would tell us of trips down the Amazon and the Andies, these were real seamen.

Whilst there I was a mate of Cliff Woodage. He was from Fleetwood. We were real mates and inseparable. I am still mates now as I write this book 58 years later. I have kept in touch with him all these years.

I was working in Leyland DAF Trucks for Securicor when I put in a request on Lancashire Radio to try to contact him. Eventually we managed to hear from his wife, Vicky, who rang to ask who I was. When I eventually saw him after twenty odd years he had not changed a bit. He still looked like the cheeky bell boy I knew on the Empress of Canada.

He was a bell hop/bell boy/lift attendance come nosy bucker and I was a commi-cook.

Cliff, now married to Vicky who is Maltese, they now live in a lovely village called St Michaels on Wyre. It's picturesque, very peaceful a real ale village, all country pubs heaven. There's a fish farm where we often stay a few nights when pissed. They have four lovely kids, two boys and two girls, Marie, Marco, Serena and Mathew. All of them extremely handsome like their mum. Only kidding! They're a credit to both of them and the children have made their mark already in their young lives. God bless.

Marco is a top man on the international motor bike circuit with his son now on board.

Marie is a top class hotel and venue manager. Serena is now making her way in the complex world of mental health and is a very lovely person.

Mathew is a God send. A lovely boy with the looks of Dean Martin, yet sadly he has a disability. But he lacks nothing and is well cared-for in the community. God bless Mathew.

Marie has the credit of being an honorary Scouser who now has letters after her. Hey LA, she is beautiful and hard-working.

Marco, like his dad, has travelled the world on the motorbike circuit and is Cliffy's double.

Serena has always been a very outgoing bubbly girl and will go far. Maybe one day she will end up living next door to Freddy Boswell out of Bread. Only kidding, God bless you all.

We're all back in touch now at this sad time for my family, but will do what Cathy would have wanted and that is to carry on and make more history.

I hope to see them all shortly after this pandemic has run its course and when I do, it's Cliffy's round.

Me and Cliffy were Vindi boys together at the camp at the same time. He passed out before me and went right to sea without going home. I recall the last weeks on the Vindi after Cliffy left.

In your last few weeks, you get to do what is called special chores, errands, etc because you're trusted. After your first six weeks or so you could do things without having to rush. For instance, in your last weeks you got to serve the officers in their mess saloon. We would wait on the captain and officers, do various duties around the camp. As privileged boys we would make up songs about new boys arriving, similar to myself six weeks previous.

It was altogether less stressful. But at the same time, I recall the last week of the Vindi, I was very nervous because of taking the final exams. The last few weeks were laid back. We were then known as pool boys and we would take the mickey of the new boys arriving each day. As it was our time to leave we got a bit cocky, but we still had to pass the final test. If we failed we would have to re-sit or be sent home. And no doubt made fun of by the other boys as we had to re-sit. If you failed again you were sent home after all that time away from home and the expense my parents had to pay.

On the day of the test I was a bag of nerves. I could not believe the outcome, little me from Greaty came third out of forty boys.

I was going to sea. I was all over the place on the last week. I was so full of it. The last day as a Vindi boy. I put on my uniform, my beret, filled my kit bag, was paid a small amount of money. I was given my train ticket and I was going home after eight weeks. I felt 6ft instead of 5ft odd.

On the journey home it was winter. I remember getting off the train and crossing for a bus outside St Georges Hall. My kit bag was bigger than me. What I must have looked like. I got on the 20 bus, I got off facing St Anthony's Church on Scotty. No-one came to meet me. I walked down Newsham Street and up Gordy. When I got to our house it was all boarded up, empty and derelict. I knocked on next door at Mrs Ryders and asked *where have they gone?*

Oh, hello Billy, said Nellie Ryder. *I never recognised you. Your mam and dad have moved to Walton Road.*

Whereabout?

Hang on Bill, 'Mam where has Jane moved to?' Luton Grove was the reply.

Thank you, I'm off.

I got the 46 bus and got off at Luton Grove, walked up the street, down the pathway and you know, it was a mansion. Four bedrooms, four gardens. As soon as I went inside, instead 'hi Bill you're home', they looked at me all togged up and laughed.

Chapter Four – First Trip to Sea and so on

After leaving the Vindi as a 16-year-old, my next step was to go right to the pool at Mann Island to sign on ready for sea. And lo and behold, I was offered a ship. It was the MV Malatian. A very small cargo boat, one of the Ellerman Pappayani fleet. The company had various ships, some small cargo, the other were city ships, much bigger. This one had a sister named the Maltasian.

After I had signed on, just after that there was a seaman's strike. Once that had finished, I was at home and suddenly there was a knock at the door. It was winter and at 4 o'clock it was dark. My mam said, *"it's for you Bill"*.

I got up and invited them in and one of the men, the chief steward, said, *"right, get your case you're off to sea"*. He was Benny Cohen, the second steward with him. I said, *"see you Mam",* and out we went to a waiting taxi, saying *ta-ra* to my mam, not dad, and other family members. It then came home to me that this is it. I won't see my dad for months. He is at work.

I was nervous but excited. On my way to sea at sixteen, we had just moved into the new house one week ago and I'm off to sea.

Once on board I was shown my cabin. As it was a small ship I had my own cabin. I was shitting it. I could feel the ship moving and loud noises outside. Well here we go, a new life. A knock came at the door. It was Benny. *"Come on Bill, here is your uniform. Put it on and follow me to the galley."*

Once in the galley I met the second cook. I knew right away I was going to be sick. We had just left the bar. It was the end of January and it was choppy. I tried to keep my feet. I met the second who asked me to clean the pans in the sink and to keep the galley tidy.

After the officers had been fed, I had to clean the saloon. I cleaned the dishes and Benny asked me to clean and set up the table in the mess as I was pantry boy as well as galley boy. Because of the size of the ship and crew, then the rest of the crew had their tea. Those on duty ate later and the bosun and those on watch were put in the oven.

Once I had met all the crew I felt less nervous. But like a fish out of water I had to take it one day at a time. The next day an early call at 5.30am, washed and ready. I was really seasick. We were in the Irish Sea and it was wild. I was strapped to the sink, could not stop being sick. After breakfast was over I could not eat a thing.

My duties as pantry boy were to clean the officers' cabins, the second steward, Benny, helped me, which took two hours, then one hour on deck. Being sick. Back in the galley and lunch, preparing spuds and vegetables.

As we went into day two, then three and four, the weather was unreal. We were in the Bay of Biscay. Be scared!

The ship was that small it moved everywhere, up, down, across, sideways. I thought we were all going to die. My first trip to sea too. After day four, while peeling spuds on deck, the weather got calmer, the sun was out and I was starting to enjoy bronzing. For a couple of hours a day I could see land all round. After five days at sea, home sick, I missed my mam and dad and brothers and little sister, but you know what I was, only sixteen, and everything in front of me was an adventure.

While on the ship I had a great mate. His name was John Kenny and he was a greaser, or donkey man, and worked down below. As he was older than me, with a family, he was around 28, he had been to sea for years, missed his family, left and then came back. This was his first trip back.

The Malatian was a friendly ship. We had Welsh, Scottish, Irish, English and Spanish and we all got on well. Because it was a small ship, John looked after me. The man John worked with below was a real Scot who could drink and the mess room was rowdy. I played darts while they drank. I was too young. We were steadily heading for Greece, our first port of call was Piraeus.

The next day it was an eye-opener. The dock was full of ships. As we were coming into the dock you could see ships from all over the world, Rotterdam, Sweden, Germany, Egypt, France, Italy, Africa. I also saw dozens of ships being scrapped. This was one of the largest ship dismantlers in the world. But I was not here for that.

Once we docked we were all ready to go ashore. Once again, John Kenny my mate, was looking after me. He was with Jock, so the three of us set off. Mr Penkelle, the skipper, said to them to look after me, *'he's only a boy'*. That never happened. Well, it did, to a degree.

It is called *Initiation*.

Once we had been in the first bar, seamen are like magnets. There are women everywhere and me being a cherry boy, I was the centre of attention. We had done most of the bars around the dock then ended up in a club. There we met the rest of the crew. They were all laughing and then next thing they were all giving money to John who was laughing.

They were speaking with some woman, and I don't mean girl, I mean woman. Two of them got hold of either of my arm, I was frog-marched up a spiral staircase, took into a room, the woman came in, shut the door. The rest is history and I lived to tell the tale ha ha.

After being thrown in the deep end my initiation was complete. No mention of the golden rivet or the Navy cake. From then on in I was one of the boys, so to speak. I was carried back to the ship.

But next morning at 5.30am call I was up ready for work. To this day I have never had a hangover. Never had a headache, bad stomach, nothing.

I don't know if the raw eggs I had on a daily basis for years along with milk beaten in a cup and then swallowed had a lot to do with it. Or could I be immune like most seamen are?

Before we left Piraeus in Greece I vowed to return. We were on our way to Beirut, another eye-opener for a young boy. The men went ashore but I was told to remain on board. It was not safe for a young boy, a dirty place, not civilised. I remained on the aft end bronzing myself till we sailed.

From Beirut we went to Latakia. Like most Arab ports it was filthy but interesting with dock workers sleeping on the dock, prostitutes, pimps, thieves, etc. I would record every port of call. Yes, I wrote it all down for future reference. I was on a journey that most boys of my age were not doing. Most would be stuck in every-day jobs mostly 9-5 office workers, while I was traveling the world, meeting people, going exotic places and all-in-all living the one life we have.

While recording all the places I promised myself one day I will enter all my knowledge, all my exploits, travel and events into a book. Well, to date, I have written five and I am only halfway to recording the journey I went on as a fifteen year old boy who, in his first few years of leaving school, had been to more places and done more things than the average man would achieve in a lifetime. How lucky I was and that is what started me off for my love of reading, writing and recording, the events of my life.

From Latakia we went to Famagusta in Cyprus. It was a lovely place. Unfortunately, Cyprus was divided by war problems but we got to see the sites and Nicosia is an awesome place.

From Cyprus we headed for Port Said in Egypt. Again, I was not recommended to go ashore at my age. A beautiful city and a wonder to behold, but not safe.

Then onto Alexandria in Egypt. The docks were booming and I saw the sites with John and Jock, hit a few bars and I traded cigarettes which I bought in the bond for my dad and his mates. I gave him two packs of Woodbines, 40, for three Egyptian carpets. They are now 57 years old and I still have them. I initially bought them for my mam which were passed back to me. Memories live forever, material things don't.

After Alexandria I was more or less homeward bound. We only had to call at Dublin then we set sail for Liverpool and home to see my mad, dad and family. When I arrived at the dock, who was on the quay to meet me? Yes, my dad and Tony Bennett, his mate. I just had to go into the salon, get paid, sign off, then re-sign for the next trip in a week's time when she was unloaded and had some repairs done.

I met my dad, gave him and Tony ciggies, tobacco and whiskey, oh and of course, a few bob. Remember I had been away six weeks at sixteen, no mobile phones, anyway my mum never had a phone. So, an adventure that took in half a dozen Mediterranean ports, that I would visit time again at sea, on holiday and by cruise ship, this is only the start. For a Vindi boy.

Chapter Five – Vindi Boys Travels

As you can see from these photographs, some in colour. Come on, it was the sixties, not your modern-day smart phone camera inclusive.

We as young 15–16-year-old boys never had the money to purchase top end camera. So whoever took these photos was certainly blessed with photographic talents.

We were either getting a bronzy on the back end, or aft end in nautical terms, or we were taking a dip in the pool. It was a makeshift pool, expertly put together by the lads themselves. How good is that? A pool increases the bronzie look, especially with salt water.

During those long months away, especially so young it was as though we were explorers because in those days suntans were only worn by men in the services. Holidays were only just getting going. So when you came home you had a bronzie. The girls would be everywhere, you were tanned, you had all the American and Canadian clothes, records and of course you had money. But mostly you were young in the sixties living the dream, going to far off lands other people could only dream of. Imagine New York, the West Indies, Canada, all the exotic parts of the world from sixteen on.

Then a new route for my next trip to maybe Italy, Spain, North Africa. This is what Vindi boys were doing all over the world. That was worth eight to twelve weeks stuck in a camp in the middle of nowhere without all your bling bling gadgets of today to communicate with the outside world. A small price to pay, though I never got over the food. It stayed with me for life.

The Vindi boys had those sorts of adventures all through the 40s, at war, the 50s, in peace time, and right up to its demise in 1967. But what an apprenticeship in life. There could be none better than to be a Vindi boy.

In these photographs obviously me and my mate Cliffy would be on a break from the galley.

His Nib on the back end in all my splendour on the Empress of Canada circa 1966-67.

Cliffy and me, shattered with no time to strip off and back to work soon.

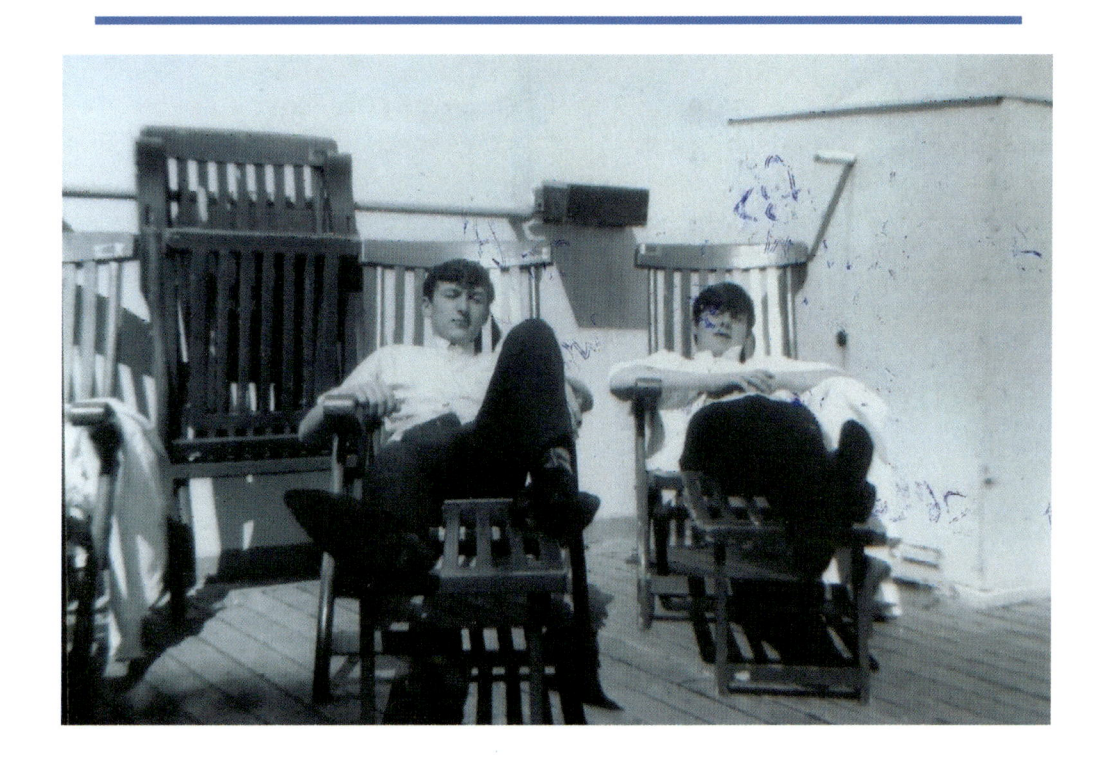

Me and a steward.

Again, asleep. Me and a steward.

Ingy Cliffy and the majestic pool.

Bum boats alongside the Empress of Canada in the West Indies while cruising.

The Empress of Canada.

Some of the lads at the backend of the pool.

Commi steward enacting on the Empress of Canada.

The Last of the Vindi Boys

We would always go topside for a break in the sunshine. Sometimes we would have an hour to strip and bronzie before going back to the galley.

The Canada had a big crew but the ratings had our own makeshift area to bunk off too. We had a pool, deckchairs, umbrellas, the lot. But we had no time to idle. We were up at 5 o'clock and in the galley by six with short breaks between sittings. So we had to be alert. We were up at 5 o'clock and working till 8-9 in the evenings, sometimes for 7 days and 9 weeks, but we were young.

Cliffy, my mate, who had the sense to retain these photographs which to date are 56 years old, he done well. And as you can see, we have not changed. Well, maybe. The hair's gone lighter and the tan is lighter. But seriously, me and Cliffy on the Empress of Canada both sixteen, two Vindi boys, it does not get better than that.

On our way to Canada or New York, or cruise the West Indies, who would believe it. But it would not come about if we had not completed our sea training in the depths of winter for those eight weeks. If we had felt home sick, if we were cold, if we missed our parents, if we were hungry, you know what, we were all of those things. But we wanted to go away to sea and nothing would stop us. It's called *'travel broadens your mind'* like nothing else on this earth.

In the photos there are other lads who we quickly formed a great bond, mostly because we were Scousers. Most were from north Liverpool, but not all. They were from Scotty, Greaty, Vauxhall, Bootle, etc. There was Eddie McCabe, Tony Delahunty, Robbie Barnes, Eddie Fullerton, Ingy and Omo. We all stuck together. It was a great time to be young.

If you want a suit length we could get it and get it made up, New York or Canada, whatever you wanted, plain, tartan, check, herring bone, pinstripe, we had them all along with the KDs, the Ben Shermans, etc, all the gear, before anyone knew they existed. We were your proverbial Liverpool Yanks.

We had our own club. Most of the lads were Vindi boys and were now proper cooks, bakers, confectioners, trainee chefs, extra chefs or indeed chefs, and all ex-Vindi boys. What a journey from Sharpness, Gloucester out in the sticks to one of the top cruise companies in the world to travel the seven seas and get paid for it. To visit every corner of the globe and all because they endeavoured to make the journey at fifteen years of age to a remote training camp in the middle of nowhere. And come what may, it was a hard institution. It was strict and it was demanding and in those days I called it for everything. It was cold, it was hard work, we were hungry.

We worked but if you ask any ex-Vindi boy today, they will tell you, that the Vindicatrix/National Sea Training School shaped them into the man they are today, and indeed more so, into the boys who were drafted from the Gravesend School before to replenish the armed forces ie merchant marines with having been torpedoed during the Second World War, carrying provisions to sustain the country.

Without the aid of the National Sea Training School the job of replacing those lost souls would not have happened and we could so easily be writing a different story. Thank God for Gravesend and Sharpness Sea Training Schools.

As boy seamen we were really well fortunate. We were the best dressed, looked tanned and healthy, had plenty of money. Put that together with a knowledge of most of the places in the world, we were made.

Chapter Six – Life Beyond the Gates

As far as the locals were concerned, those of that opinion were inclined to think that the boys at the Vindi camp were naughty boys. But nothing was further from the truth.

A lot of the local people would entertain the boys when they were out and about in Berkeley. The boys would attend church regularly. The locals would know these boys were away from home, some very lonely and homesick and not always treated well.

A lot of the local men were jealous of the boys. They thought they were pinching their girls. Well, I have to say that did happen, but it takes two to tango. It was a quiet part of the world and what few girls that were around were spoilt for choice. Just like when the Yanks arrived in the UK. And most of the girls were spoilt for choice and most of the local boys were dull to them when they had Scousers being cheeky to them and having a laugh.

The boys came from everywhere: Glasgow, Wales, Newcastle, London, etc. The girls were spoilt and they knew it because there was not many to be had.

So there may have been some trouble, you know what teenagers are like, if there is conflict, especially if they are all speaking a different dialect. We were not drinking alcohol, there was fights but they had to put all that to bed before returning to camp. If we were caught fighting then all the boys involved would be sent home, not just one. Any other skirmish you were under the clock or had to see the skipper, but they were strict but fair. Thank God.

We would often go to the pictures in Berkeley. Outside that there was the Flying Angel where we could play pool, have a snack. Bu apart from that there was not much. There was one girl who would knock around each day at the club but she was no lady ha ha, so nobody bothered. I think her name was Jasper, I don't know why.

Apart from the Gospel Hall there was not much going on. I have to say at the time it was an experience I just wanted to get the best out of. The good points were I met lots of mates from all over the UK. I met my mate Cliffy, experienced all things nautical and ate some of the worst food in my life.

The Vindi boys now are thin on the ground. Remember we were fifteen 57 years ago and those before me will now be near eighty.

So because me and Cliffy were part of the last intake, I think that we are still compos mentis and my brain, now along with my other functions, are still working. Yes, I still attend the reunions, not last year because of the Covid situation, but I will go this year if only to see how many of us are left.

The Vindi closed in 1968 so if you base that on my age, come on we're not far off extinction. That's why it's important to keep the memory alive.

It's sad when you think the average Vindi boy who may well never had been to a reunion in Sharpness could exit this world not knowing that they are part of history. The Vindi boys were an exceptional group of young men from all backgrounds who descended on Sharpness in their hundreds of thousands from 1928 onwards, from Gravesend, Kent, then from Sharpness.

From the National Sea Training Schools from all over the UK, be in war time or peace time, if it was not for the enormous amount of research done by Roy Derham the Vindi Sea Training School could easily have been passed in history.

Roy Derham brought the Vindi and its boys back to life, literally, and to the attention of today.

I tried in my own city of Liverpool to re-ignite the Vindi boys but the powers that be said who or what significance is the ship the Vindicatrix to Liverpool Museum, ie Maritime. Their answer was why would we do an exhibition on the Vindicatrix when it is not a Liverpool registered ship, not a Liverpool located training school, has no local connections. Sorry.

The Gravesend School of National Sea Training was one of the schools before the Vindi relocated from East India Dock in Gravesend to Sharpness in 1939. Since then while replenishing the war effort with thousands of young boys, mainly from Liverpool, Wirral and the North West, these boys died while crewing ships in the Atlantic, carrying provisions in convoys that were torpedoed by submarines. And from the Vidicatrix relocating to Sharpness, a great majority of the boys were from the North West, mostly Liverpool. So why is it not of interest to Liverpool Museum?

There was always Vindi boys meeting each month in Liverpool in the Liverpool Arms, Eldonian Village Hall, etc. A man, ex-Vindi boy, Charles Boyd, was a great ambassador for the Vindi boys. Thanks Charles.

Charles has sadly passed away but I intend to keep it going by writing about it locally.

There was once a programme on BBC Radio Merseyside when Vindi boys told their stories to Angela Heslop, I believe. It somehow fizzled out even though they said they would rekindle it. I mentioned it to a member of BBC Radio Merseyside, Roger Phillips, a few years back, who was always on the side of the people being recognised for their efforts. I will endeavour in my own way to keep the Vindi boys in touch with the media as much as I can.

The Vindicatrix has been scrapped yet the Vindi boys, even now, is very much alive with a story to tell and I will go on beating my drum. I will attend this year's reunion at Sharpness on 5-7 August 2021. I will not be shut up. There is a story to tell.

So if the Museum will not show it, then I will write about it in my own words as a story worth telling. It is, if you like, any fifteen year old going off to war. He does not know what to expect. He does not know where he is going. So why would you not want to display some sort of message? Why not a plaque? A statue might be a bit too much, after all Sharpness has one outside the gates of the camp and it was unveiled by none other than the captain of Queen Elizabeth II whose father before him was captain of the QEII, both ex-Vindi boys and both from Wallasey.

Their names are Captain Warwick Senior and Junior. So you see you have captains of great ships from Merseyside who trained at the Sea Training School but it does not warrant a mention in the neck of the woods they were born. How strange.

Chapter Seven – Use It Or Lose It

When you have been a part of nautical history when Liverpool as a port is known the world over, our maritime history was once the major port in the world when all our riches, houses, buildings, parks, etc were built on commerce. When our docks were the busiest in the world, our dockers the most famous, our ships, be it every cruise vessel in the world called here, every building was a shipping office, every company wanted Liverpool as their place of registry. Cunard, Canadian Pacific, PNC, Harrisons, Ellerman, Pappyani, Bibby Lines, Elder Dempster. I can go on yet even the slave trade played some part be it small, mostly ship ownership. It's a maritime city with one of the most iconic rivers and waterfronts in the world. I would know, I have been to most of them.

As a Vindi boy I cannot get my head around why the great and the good of this city do not commemorate the Vindi. We know it was not a Liverpool ship, it never sailed out of Liverpool. Well that would be a miracle the shape it was in. It was a training vessel. She is not a ship of the day, yet, it has Liverpool ties in its trainees.

They, each year, were made in numbers by Scousers, and plastic Scousers. I feel as time goes by we can lose it. Give it 20 years there will be no-one left to recall and say, *yes I am a Vindi boy*. It will have passed. But like a lot of things in life you must have heard it.

Yes, he was a good man, or yes, it was a great film, or he done wonder in his life and talk about something or someone who has gone. Why not recognise the person, the building, the ship, etc, while it is in the present?

The Vindicatrix has not been forgotten in Sharpness itself. Each year, apart from Covid, they hold a reunion. All ex-Vindi boys go, not all from around the world, some from Tasmania, their gather at Sharpness Docks or on the site of the former school.

On the old site were the Vindi was berthed now lies a boating marina, very appropriate. I believe the current site is owned by United Utilities. There are stalls of bric-a-brac, memorabilia, and of course food and drink in the Dockers Club. Loads of photographs of the boys and group ones of the year you were there, all-in-all it's a great weekend. It's normally early August. They come from all corners of the world, all ex-Vindi boys with now powerful and prestigious titles, etc. Again, without the foresight of Roy I may not be writing this book.

My book does not dwell on the Vindi boys the way Roy Derham's did. He did it on a national and international scale. Mine is purely to do with the small amount of Vindi boys I know personally and those located to my place of birth, Liverpool.

But in Sharpness, the fact that a packed house can turn up each year, I am not sure what we will get this year, but I will comment on it at the end of the book, ref Covid. But all-in-all we have enough Vindi boys still standing to make a noise so I do not want to leave this world without this mission being accomplished. I am in a small way through the Vindi boys included in this book, making our existence known.

For whatever reason, Liverpool City Council, The Heritage Board, the Sea Training Establishment, choose to ignore we're here and as much part of Liverpool maritime history. It does astound me to think we have been forgotten or ignored.

How can thousands of Liverpool and Wirral men go to a training school outside Liverpool, go to sea school in Sharpness with the history the Vindicatrix had, then sent to sea to replenish the war effort, to replace the massive scale of human life lost at sea.

As well as trying to contain the precious cargoes they were carrying to keep people fed and sustain the war effort, those boys never went to sea schools to be German fodder. Were they to know what would face them no, but they had a purpose which was well documented. Their reason for joining the sea school was to be a seaman to travel the world, to experience life, new friends, places, not to die within days of leaving the school.

Not to have seen their parents, to have that thrill of saying yes, I went to the Vindicatrix and Gravesend at 15, yes I trained with thousands of boys from everywhere, yes I passed and became a seaman. How proud that boy's parents had been for their son to become a man overnight and then only to be killed at sea of a terrible death. To be sunk by a German U-boat. Was that the purpose of want to join the sea training school? No.

It was to go to sea firstly, and thousands achieved that dream once the war was over and to do in life what they signed up for at the pool. The Vindi, up until the middle to late 60s when the inevitable would happen, my pleas have always fell on stony ground yet I will try to get some recognition for those that perished that were part of the sea schools. The sea training schools were institutions that gave boys from all backgrounds the opportunity to go to sea. A very worthwhile and fulfilling ambition for any

15 year old and in Liverpool, like myself, whose father and grandfather were seamen, a realisation of achieving that dream.

Over the years there have been many people who have kept the Vindi dream alive. Roy Derham started the ball rolling and done a wonderful job of rekindling the Vindi boys all over the world and was suitably honoured for his efforts by HM The Queen. Nearer home, a man who was a Vindi boy, also a tireless campaigner for the Vindi, was Charles Boyd who done so much to keep the name alive. Charles was paramount in setting up meetings, social nights, local reunions and so on. Sadly, Charles passed away but I always recall his name on Merchant Navy Day and I feel that with the passing of time I and the remainder of the Vindi boys will go off the radar. But I can do no more to pursue a dream for eight weeks to travel to a far-off land, if you like, than to go to sea. But in times of war, the history books will remember the Second World War but will they remember the boys from the sea training school who have trained to replenish the men already lost? I doubt it.

But my purpose in writing this book which has been a pleasure and an honour as I am a Vindi boy is to bring to light to what has been ignored by the historians and try to keep the memory alive of all those boys who did their best in the sea school and in war and peace. Some went on to do great things, like Roy. Some perished in war but we must not forget we were all trained by the National Sea Training Schools.

Chapter Eight – Future Recognition

The very purpose of this book is not just to establish that I, William Henry Booth Jnr, as a Vindi boy who trained at Sharpness, Gloucester at 15, now gives me the status of being a Vindi boy, but to try in a small way by writing about it, the instructors, the discipline, the weather, the food, the ship, but all those points that makes you want to go to sea as a young boy,

But actually being there and being part of that time in history when sea training was done all over the UK by various companies, all training their own boys. Yet somehow the Vindi strikes a bigger chord, you're part of something, not just a ship but a family of Vindi boys. Sadly, no girls.

And in a small way through the book make someone stand up and say, *hang on, who are the Vindi boys, what do they represent what have they done where have they been?*

To put it in perspective, it's like demolishing a building of real interest, a building that had character, that had been part of our lives for years, a true landmark, and then saying why did we demolish it? It could have stayed, it could have been a massive tourist attraction for years.

That's how I feel about the Vindicatrix. It was a ship that had a great history yet it was scrapped. Why?

The remaining Vindi boys will forever remember and try, like me, to give an account to future generations that the Vindicatrix was not just a lump of metal, it was an institution and to be part of that, along with thousands of other boys, we are now known as the last of the Vindi boys.

Chapter Nine – Vindi Boys Stories Circa 1965-66

Cliffy Woodage, my mate, was at the Vindi in 1965-66 scrubbing the decks, running around the parade ground, up at 6am each morning.

Cliffy Woodage

Every day it was cold. I was there in winter for two months, the first thing they told me was put on weight or you will not last out.

Mum would send food parcels, we would not survive otherwise. Some boys would train as deckhands. I was in the catering department. It seemed to go on forever. I was 15 years old and most of them were the same.

I joined my first ship, a passenger liner. It was massive. The Empress of Canada from Liverpool. We went to New York and the Caribbean for three months, came back to Liverpool then off to Canada and made that crossing regular. I met Billy on board. He had left the Vindi six months before we met. Instead of going home we would all stay at Bill's house in Walton. Then the winkle pickers would go on and we were off to the Cavern.

The Beatles were on the scene in those days. It was a happy time when we were young, tanned, loaded, fresh-faced. The good times and good days. We all had the world at our feet and all the world to see.

Sometimes we would go down Scotty Road for a drink. It was the best time ever. I have given Bill some photos of us on the Empress of Canada. We were both catering boys back then.

I left the Empress after one year. Billy got in touch with me after a few years and I still get in touch now.

My next ship was the Pacific Northwest. We would sail the west coast of America. I stayed on board for one and a half years. Then three month trips after that. I joined a ship call the Temple Lane. Six to seven days at sea at 9 knots from Sweden to Communist China, Moa Tse-Tung, Red Guards, guns in turrets and all that. Some of the crew had a bad time from the guards. The trip was six months.

My last ship was Gron Breatter Beacon, a tramp steamer. The trip was a year long and included the Philippines, copra lights in coconut for the oil. We would go to San Francisco and back to the Philippines for a whole year and then we would fly home.

I could have bought a house but I blew it on booze. That's life, best years of my life looking back. All seamen will have stories to tell. There were very few planes in those days. Life was basic, Billy still rings me. That's a good friend.

- Clive Woodage, a Vindi Boy forever.

Comments

Just imagine the life my mate Cliffy had in those days. He would visit places most people have not heard of. What a journey for a young man.

- Bill Booth

Mick O'Toole, Liverpool, circa 1959

I am 79 years old and joined the Vindi in 1959 at the age of 17. It was my first time away from home and we were to do six weeks' training and four weeks' maintenance work.

The training mainly consisted of instructions of knots compass recognition, steering, always repeat the order, boat rowing and general duties. It was mostly interesting and enjoyable. One lad in our intake thought by us to be of mixed race was to turn out to be a gypsy who never washed so was packed off home before the end of the first week.

Though the lads came from all parts of the country it was soon obvious that sizeable a Scouse contingent ran the show.

We were based in barracks with one officer in residence to keep an eye on us all. Each Saturday was spent cleaning the hut from top to bottom. A prize of a cake was awarded each week to the cleanest hut after inspection and we won it one week.

I was a music nutter even at that age and the first month went by without any radio or media. On the fourth Saturday as we cleaned away our officer left his room door open and his radio on. The first thing we heard was "What do you want" by Adam Faith.

Mr Scott was Chief Officer at the time who we always found to be very straight and fair. He took us for all our knots. The only one I remember is a reef knot. Another, whose name sadly I can't recall, always referred to as 'Popeye' would sometimes rouse us in the morning, banging loudly on the hut door, shouting 'hands off cocks on with the socks'. One of our Irish contingents fancied himself as a tattoo artist. Most seafarers at the time would have the two bluebirds just behind their thumbs.

Foolishly, I let him have a go with a needle and Indian ink which gave me blood poisoning. He did turn out to be good at art and when we were issued with our kit bags, was in demand for painting either Popeye or a mermaid on them.

I settled for a mermaid but never used the bag again. We had plenty of shore time over the weeks and happily took advantage of the local seaman's mission to break the tedium. They supplied tea, cold drinks and pies to us young lads, making us feel right at home. The time seemed to pass very quickly and my ten weeks were soon up.

Prior to enlisting on the Vindi I was courting a young girl called Shirley. We wrote back and forth while I was away.

My hair tended to be longer than most at the time and having been pre-warned had a haircut before going. Sadly for me, I still had to endure two more haircuts while down there.

First Saturday back I had to report to the famous Mr Brown at the pool, down by the Pier Head. This had to be done in the full dreadful uniform we had endured for the full ten weeks.

I was doing my best to avoid the lovely Shirley seeing me in that rig and with an awful haircut. Coming back from the pool, who should be on the bus, but Shirley. That was the end of that little romance.

A couple of weeks home and I was posted to the Empress of France. The exact date escapes me, but we were at sea on Christmas Day in 1959 when the crew was served our dinner by the officers, an old Navy tradition and quite an experience for a 17 year old. The first two days of our trip had seen us four deck boys, prostrate in our bunks, badly seasick till the third day when we were rudely kicked out of our bunks by the duty officer and made to turn to.

I had signed on for six trips on the France. The old 21 day turnaround which meant St John, New Brunswick and Montreal and Quebec when the St Lawrence seaway cleared.

My maternal grandfather had drowned off the Empress of Ireland and I was to pass the very site of the tragedy several times.

On either the third or fourth trip we were caught in a tremendous gale in mid-Atlantic on 12-4 watch. We were eating dinner when the ship heeled right over, hurling us our dinner and the dishes to the floor. A couple of broken arms and wrists ensued but I escaped any injury.

Our fourth officer was to tell later how he was shaving prior to coming on watch and looking out the porthole saw the France go so far over he doubted if it would come back. He had been 30 years at sea and knew his stuff. Our plight was well reported in the media which gave the folks at home some concern.

Supposedly I was due for six trips but prior to sailing on the sixth, I was found to be drunk in Dutch Eddies and missed the sailing from the Gladstone Dock.

While home I went to work with a mate in a wholesale butchers at the back of the Locarno and never went back. I well realise that most of the seaman I've known were longer at sea on one trip than I was in my entire career, but it was certainly an experience and mostly enjoyable.

Just a few memories shared.

- Mick O'Toole

Comments

I have to say Mick, that what you experienced alone while navigating the Bell Isle Straits, the St Lawrence in winter and while enjoying the Lakes and principal sights of Canada, along with your 90 degree list could not have been achieved anywhere else. Real memories.

Charlie May, circa 1951-52

Charlie went to the Vindi in 1951-52 for about 12 weeks. Some of his mates were Butch Bodesa (who appears behind him in the photo), Sammy Curtis (Butch's mate), John McIvor from Wirral, Kenny Twidale, a lad named Smith (he was from London).

I went in the boxing ring twice with him when they had no boxing matches the first Monday of the week. I also went in with John McIvor.

We were always hungry. A couple of us would walk along the railway to a small town called Berkeley, to the mission. We would get a mug of cocoa and a sandwich. We used to pinch a couple of loaves when they delivered the bread to the Vindi. I was glad when the 12 weeks were up and over with. In our last two weeks after we finished training we were put to work laying a path in a field.

In the field was an old barn. We went in and there were two barrels full of fermenting cider. One of the Scots lads had a go at it and we ended up bringing him back in a wheelbarrow. We held him up while the mail got called out. Lucky there was no mail for him that day.

Photograph of Charlie May and his billet – barracks 1951-52.

Comments

Charlie you have not changed. I knew one day you were destined for the docks in Garston. Nice one mate.

- W H Booth Jnr (Billy)

Prominent Vindi Boys

John Prescot was at the Vindi. He sailed to sea as a ship steward. Also Tommy Steele and his brother were at the Vindi

Vindi Boy Bill Booth, circa 1965-66

I have to say the Vindi shaped me. I was fifteen away from home for eight weeks, that would be unheard of today. You would have to leave your mobile phone behind, no comfortable beds, no telly till three in the morning, no Deliveroos, no Just Eat. I mean the Navy would be short of men to crew those ships. It would not happen.

We were kids in unknown territory deep in the heart of Bristol, Gloucestershire, in the sticks. If you could not stand the pace you would have to go AWOL. We were up at 5.30am on parade in pumps and shorts, t-shirts in the winter. No electric blankets. But it made us what we are today.

Most seamen do not have a problem with a few hours sleep. It was hard but we survived.

The Vindi Top Three Specials

1. The Vindi Loo

No this is not a curry. It is an alfresco bog. The only one on the River Severn and it just happens to be on the quay, right facing the ship. To be honest, it could have been in Beirut it was that bad. The smell you could bottle and it would be ideal in any war zone or used as fresh air spray on the Vindi to get rid of the cockroaches.

2. The Vindi Roll

It was a form of sponge cake, full of raisins and sultanas and it was the only meal I looked forward to. It was encased in a tin coffin then steamed. When the jacket was opened it was the best steam pudding for miles and great with custard. I hope a café in Berkely have the menu.

3. The Vindi Song

> Bless them all, bless them all
> The long and the short and the tall
> Bless all the bosuns and their bosuns mates
> Bless all the new boys and their empty plates
> Because we're saying goodbye to them all
> It's back to their billets they crawl
> They'll get no promotion this side of the ocean
> So come back on, bless them all

Chapter Ten – Vindicatrix, The History

The ship was launched in 1989 at Port Glasgow and named *The Arranmore*, a fully rigged ship she was, 1,946 tons of pure steel, she hit 3,300 tons. She was a strong ship and she looked the part.

She had a great history of the world of shipping, carrying coal and even wheat. She had a great deal of accidents during her time at sea.

There was a bad accident in South Africa in early 1903 and at some point after that, enough was enough and she was sold. Believe it or not, to a German company who bought her in 1909.

From then on she was re-named and she became *Waltraute*. She would carry on trading and mostly she would carry the same type of cargo she was used to over the years, ie wheat etc. She continued to trade for some years and then she had another stroke of bad luck and would run into bad weather when she was just leaving a port in South Africa. She was left with bad damage to her rigging system and they would have to find a port to rest and wait for the weather to clear. They made for Montevideo and she rested there for a while before eventually setting sail to make her way back to Germany.

Later, she would reach Germany and make for Hamburg and would then be sold on again to the Sea Dock Council. Again, she would live to see another day. She was commissioned by the German Navy.

Later on she would end up on her way to the Baltic and again, another twist and turn to her career, where she would go on to become a training ship for the German Navy to train u-boat crew cadets.

After the First World War she would once again move onto Leith where she would end up serving German seamen, those that were being re-patriated.

Again luck was not with her. She would be involved in several scrapes and unfortunately bad weather. She would constantly meet bad weather. She then had the misfortune of running into the docks.

Unfortunately she would have the misfortune of having to be salvaged. The ultimate stroke of bad luck that followed her since her first day at sea.

Eventually down the line she would be sold to, guess who, yes the Shipping Federation. All-in-all she would find her way to the East India

Dock where she would lay for a while before her fate was decided. She would remain there where she would take on all manner of tasks. She would have to go through the indignity of having to be renamed again. This time luck was on her side and with this new name she would find her place in history and become the Vindicatrix.

Yes, it could possibly be her last berth, but no, this ship keeps evolving. She was later moved from the East India to a berth in Gravesend, Kent which is where she would stay for some time to fulfil her loyal commission.

Forever the hulk Vindicatrix, a former sailing ship of 2,000 tons, served her time at Gravesend after being in the East India Docks. In 1926 she was commissioned to help accommodate and train pupils. She would do this for years before making what we now know was her last move, on Thursday 8th June 1939, the Vindicatrix was towed from Gravesend, Kent to Sharpness Docks. There she would accommodate and train pupils in all aspects of sea going skills in order to enable the trainees to go to sea, be it as a steward, waiter, winger, cook or deck hand recruit.

The Vindicatrix would go on and continue to trade, if you like, for another twenty eight years, plus steadily suppling fresh recruits for the war effort and in peace time replenishing and training thousands of young boys to help the keep the ships manned and would have aboard their ships the most qualified young merchant seamen. They all trained and turned out to be a polite and all wanting to maintain the traditions of the Merchant Navy and to become a glowing example of the manner in which they were trained.

By all those dedicated officers and staff at the National Sea Training School, ie the Vindicatrix, The Vindi, God bless you all.

She would go on to train thousands of young boys from the heady days of the Merchant Navy Reserve Pool where the boys would report after training to the various pools, be it wherever they were in the country to be moved onto various ships. Hence the name *Pool Boys* who were in their last week of training on the Vindicatrix before leaving for sea life. The Sea Federation would supply the boys to the type of ship they were suited by the report would have from the Sea School.

Above, where the Vindicatrix was moored 2021.
Below, the Vindi loo, alongside the boats on the quay, 2021

Sharpness today, 2021

The River Severn in all her glory.

More views of where it all began, today.

What's left of the camp.

What's left of the billets and barracks where we were housed during those very harsh winter months.

Chapter Eleven – The 2021 Vindicatrix Reunion at Sharpness

I have to start with the man who made it all possible, the man who had the vision to go on a journey literally and bring together the Vindi boys. A quest he started in the 1990s which culminated in a now extensive amount of Vindi boys from this country and as far as Australia, at least another four or five countries, and indeed nationally and every year for the last twenty or so years, a reunion annually at the Dockers Blub on Sharpness Dock, next to the Sea School. Roy worked his magic and was awarded the MBE. What an achievement.

Thank you, Roy.

Roy Derham, founder and saviour to all the Vindi boys. This is Roy and author Bill Booth at the 2021 Reunion

In 2003 the monument was erected and unveiled by the Captain of the QE2, Captain Warwick, on the site of the Sea Training School in Sharpness in memory of the Vindicatrix and the 70,000 boys who trained there from 1939 to 1967. What a day, I along with my friend, Cliffy Woodage, Vicky and Cathy, were also present. We had a ball.

Photos of the monument unveiled in 2003. The monument representing two ships intertwined.

Photos of the monument unveiled in 2003. The monument representing two ships intertwined.

The plaque outside the infamous Vindi loo, the only al fresco loo on the River Severn.

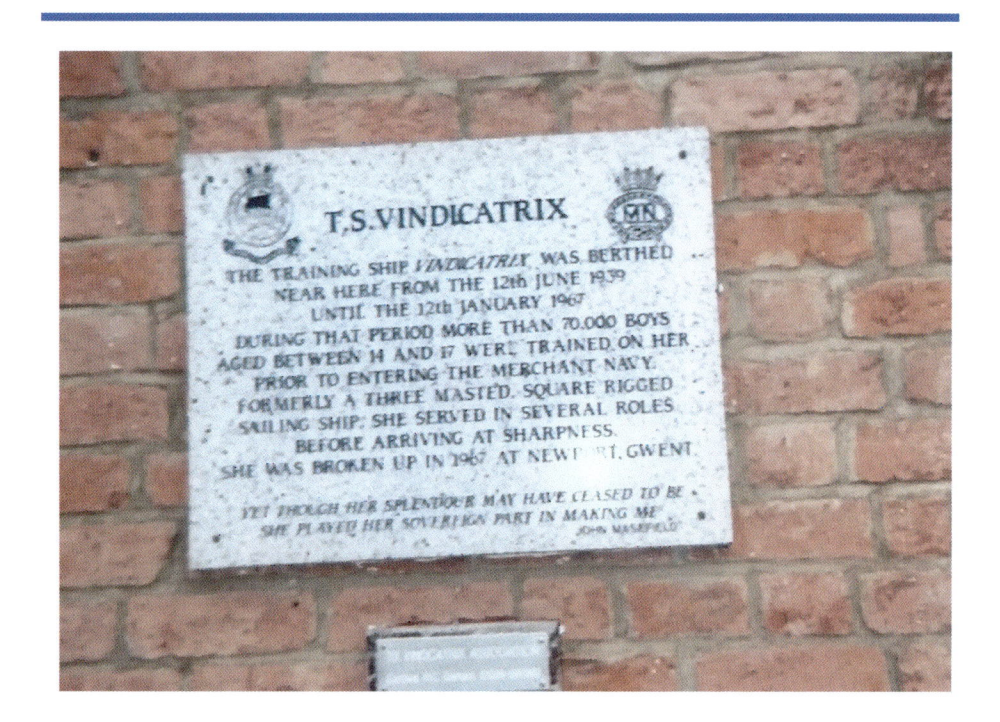

Berkeley Village, today.

Where the Vindi boys would go to the cinema at weekends and would visit the mission hall on Sundays for church service. Afterwards they would be served tea and tab nabs by the local ladies of Berkeley. Unfortunately the cinema has gone and now a garage. The mission hall has been rebuilt.

Closing with a few more shots of the demolished sea school site in Sharpness.

A detail of my Red Book after leaving the Vindi for sea.

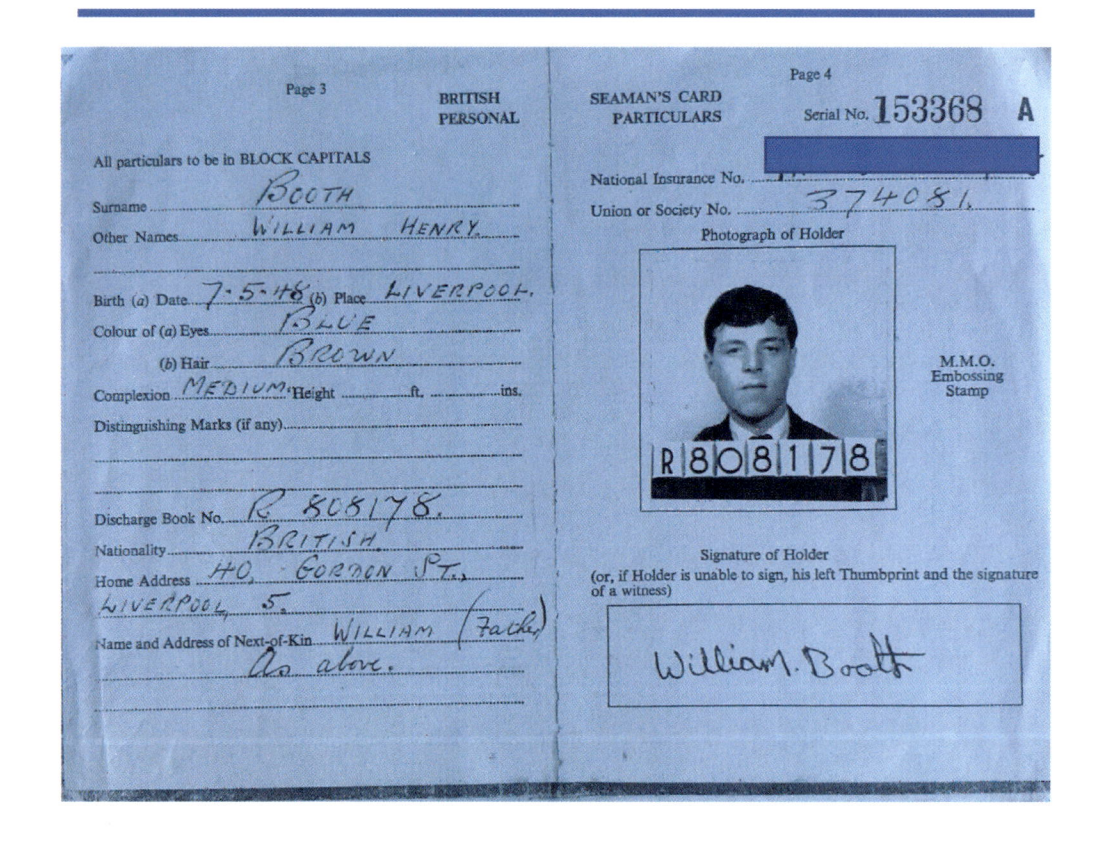

Vindy boys through the years.

The Last of the Vindi Boys

THIS MONUMENT
WAS ERECTED
BY THE
T.S. VINDICATRIX
ASSOCIATION
AND UNVEILED ON
9th AUGUST 2003
BY
Captain R W WARWICK

The Last of the Vindi Boys

For sale on Amazon

All royalties go to the three charities that both Bill and Cathy have supported for years and years.

**Part 1 of a trilogy
In Reach of St Polycarps**

**Part 2 of a trilogy
Liverpool 5 – Salt of the Earth**

**Part 3 of a trilogy
The Boothies – She Laughed More Than She Cried**

Liverpool Back In The Day

The Last of the Vindi Boys

Books to come …

**No Ordinary Woman
(a biography of Catherine Mary Booth)**

**Here You Go, Billy: One Life
(autobiography of William Henry Booth Jnr)**

**All books now available on Amazon or telephone +44 (0) 151 427 4161, +44 (0) 151 547 2752, +44 (0) 151 475 2903
Also available at Jermaines One or
Email: janey248@gmail.com**

Printed in Great Britain
by Amazon